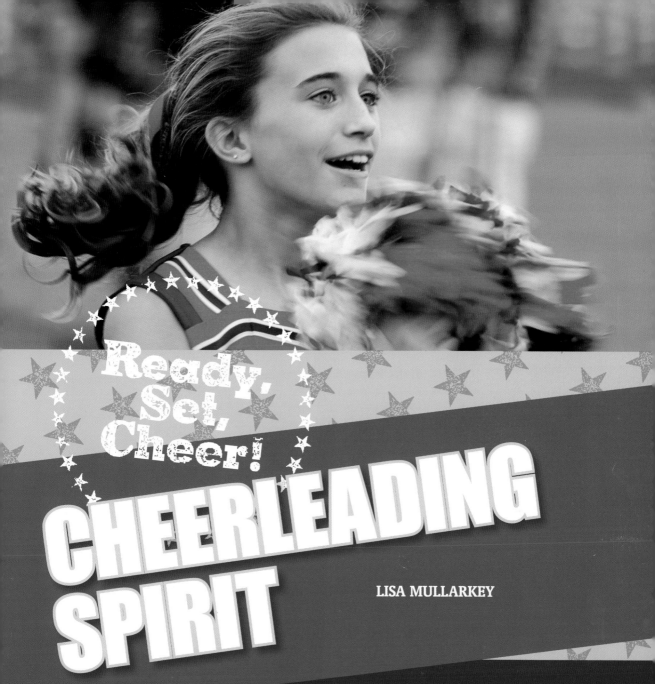

Ready, Set, Cheer!

CHEERLEADING SPIRIT

LISA MULLARKEY

Enslow Publishers, Inc.
40 Industrial Road
Box 398
Berkeley Heights, NJ 07922
USA

http://www.enslow.com

Many thanks to Emily Beggiato, Erika Lipinski, Alyssa Materazzo,
Abby Michta, Sarah Mullarkey, and Bryanna Papcun
for their contributions to this book.
Special thanks to Steven DeCasperis for a number of the photos used here.

Copyright © 2011 by Enslow Publishers, Inc.

Library of Congress Cataloging-in-Publication Data

Mullarkey, Lisa.
      Cheerleading spirit / Lisa Mullarkey.
            p. cm. — (Ready, set, cheer!)
      Includes bibliographical references and index.
      Summary: "Readers will learn about the power of positive attitudes,
pep rallies, and spirit"—Provided by publisher.
            ISBN 978-0-7660-3538-6
            1. Cheerleading—Juvenile literature. I. Title.
      LB3635.M85 2010
      791.6′4—dc22   2009037239

ISBN-13: 978-1-59845-199-3 (paperback)

Printed in the United States of America

052010 Lake Book Manufacturing, Inc., Melrose Park, IL

10 9 8 7 6 5 4 3 2 1

To Our Readers: We have done our best to make sure all Internet addresses in this book were active
and appropriate when we went to press. However, the author and the publisher have no control over
and assume no liability for the material available on those Internet sites or on other Web sites they
may link to. Any comments or suggestions can be sent by e-mail to comments@enslow.com or to the
address on the back cover.

♻ Enslow Publishers, Inc., is committed to printing our books on recycled paper. The paper in every
book contains 10% to 30% post-consumer waste (PCW). The cover board on the outside of each book
contains 100% PCW. Our goal is to do our part to help young people and the environment too!

Illustration Credits: Associated Press, pp. 28, 33, 35, 38; courtesy of Steven DeCasperis, pp. 4, 6, 7;
Nicole diMella/Enslow Publishers, pp. 11, 12, 22, 24, 25, 36, 45; © Michelle Malven/iStockphoto.com,
p. 1; © Andrew Rich/iStockphoto.com, p. 20; Shutterstock.com, pp. 9, 15, 17, 18, 29, 30, 34, 39, 41, 43,
44, 45.

Cover Illustration: © Michelle Malven/iStockphoto.com.

CONTENTS

When spirits are down, bring on the cheerleaders!

1
ATTITUDE IS EVERYTHING

Your team is down in the dumps after losing a game. Fans would rather buy snacks at the stand than watch the game. The morale at school is low. Across town, the mayor is worried that the kickoff event for the new library will be boring.

What should you do?

Call the cheerleaders!

Why? Cheerleaders are able to lift everyone's spirit! It is the cheerleaders' job to get the crowd excited. Their enthusiasm is contagious. Cheerleaders spread their spirit at games, pep rallies, and community events.

Show Your Spirit!

All cheerleaders have spirit, but what is it? Spirit is showing pride in your team, your school, your community, and

Great cheerleaders have spirit as well as skills.

yourself. You can see, feel, and hear it. It is the swoosh of electricity that buzzes through the air. It is the chatter in the stands before the game. It is the chants and cheers. Spirit soars when fans wear the team's colors from head to toe. It rises when they paint their faces. Your job as a cheerleader is to help spread the spirit with your positive attitude.

What does a positive attitude have to do with cheerleading? Everything! Good cheerleaders can land jumps and fly through the air with ease. But *great* cheerleaders have the whole package: skills *and* a winning attitude! It is the cheerleaders with A+ attitudes that coaches want on their teams.

Harvard University Head Cheerleading Coach Kristin Capasso agrees. "Many coaches would rather pick the hardworking weaker athlete with the great attitude over the talented know-it-all that could care less," she says.

Your job as a cheerleader is to help spread the spirit.

Capasso should know. She sees many talented cheerleaders every year at tryouts. She says:

> One year, a girl stood out because she took the time to find me during her pre-freshman fair in the spring. She found me again during Freshman Orientation in September. I could tell she was eager to be on the team.
>
> However, when she performed her skills during tryouts, it was clear that her skills were limited. Despite her weaknesses in the basics and her lack of experience, there was something about her drive. Her enthusiasm and eagerness to be on our squad drew me to her. Although she did not demonstrate all the required skills, I put her on the team.
>
> By the end of our season, she was awarded the Most Improved on the team. She became one of my most dedicated and talented cheerleaders. Attitude and desire are the most important factors in deciding who will become a Harvard Crimson cheerleader.

What's Your 'Tude?

Do you have an A+ attitude? Take this quiz to find out.

★ *Do you get frustrated if you cannot master a move right away?* A+ Attitude Answer: Of course not! You know that practice makes perfect. An A+ attitude means never giving up.

★ *Your tumbling is terrific, but a teammate is having a hard time. Will you offer to help her?* A+ Attitude Answer: You bet! All for one, and one for all! Part of having a winning attitude is stepping up to be a leader when one is needed.

★ *Do you get upset if your coach changes your favorite routine?* A+ Attitude Answer: Why get upset? The coach looks out for the whole team. Maybe a stunt was too dangerous. You go with the flow!

★ *Do you work on your skills every day?* A+ Attitude Answer: Absolutely! Practice makes the routines look sharp and polished.

★ *Do you complain when your coach says, "One more time"?* A+ Attitude Answer: Never! The coach is in charge. Smile, give 110%, and set a good example.

Did you make the honor roll? You did if you had an A+ attitude!

Jump Off on the Right Foot!

The key to a successful squad is a team's spirit. In order for the spirit to soar, the team has to bond and work well together. It does not mean you must become best

Great moves are important. An A+ attitude is essential!

friends with your teammates. It means that you should get to know, care about, trust, and respect them. Team bonding takes time. A great way to get a jump start on making friends at the beginning of the year is to do activities together. Try the following to pump up the spirit!

Spirit Bags

Decorate a brown lunch bag in team colors, using markers or paint. Punch holes in the four corners of the bag. Push curling ribbon through each hole. Tie ribbons into a knot and curl using scissors. Put items listed below into the bag. At the first practice, pass the bags out. Each person takes a turn pulling an item out of the bag and tries to guess its meaning.

- ★ *Paper snowflake:* Everyone is special and unique.
- ★ *Star:* You shine and should reach for the stars.
- ★ *Penny:* You are a valuable part of the team.
- ★ *Gold thread:* Our friendship and spirit tie our hearts together.
- ★ *Pipe cleaner:* Stretch to stay flexible.
- ★ *Eraser:* We all make mistakes.
- ★ *Puzzle piece:* The squad would not be complete without you.
- ★ *Happy face sticker:* Smile, smile, smile!
- ★ *Sponge:* Soak up the coach's tips.

- ★ *Popsicle stick:* Stick your stunts and stick together through good and bad times.

- ★ *Rubber band:* Snap your motions.

- ★ *Balloon:* Keep spirits inflated.

- ★ *Glove:* Give someone a helping hand when needed.

- ★ *Starburst candy:* For when you need a burst of energy.

- ★ *Paper doily:* We look delicate on the outside, but we are strong and tough on the inside.

SPREAD THE SPIRIT:

Write the quotes from this book on your bags.

Games

Playing games can make people feel comfortable. They "break the ice" and allow everyone to get to know each other.

1. Find the Fake: Everyone shares three statements about themselves. Two are true. One is made up. Your teammates try to guess which fact is the fake.

2. Mix and Mingle: Divide squad into groups of two. Each pair gets a card with questions on it. Everyone must talk to the other groups to find the answers. Your coach should put the questions together. Here are some to get started:

In order for a squad to be great, members need to bond and work together.

- ★ Name three people who share the same birthday month.

- ★ Who is left-handed?

- ★ Who lives closest to the high school?

- ★ Who has the most brothers and sisters?

- ★ Name five people who can do a back handspring.

TIP: Have everyone write down one funny fact about herself. Have your coach include them in the questions. Example: Find the person who loves ketchup on her pancakes.

3. Team Talk: New squad members might feel nervous at practice. Help them out! Pair new cheerleaders with returning cheerleaders. Set aside time at the end of each practice to talk, create new cheers and chants, and make posters for the game.

4. Wrap it Up! End the first week of practice on a high note. Write down everyone's first name on separate pieces of paper. Sit in a circle and pass out a piece of paper to each member of your squad. Everyone will have a different name on her paper. Each person has one minute to write a positive message or a compliment to that person. After a minute, everyone passes her paper to the right. Write another message or compliment to the new girl. At the end, give each girl the paper with her name. Everyone goes home with a page full of inspirational messages!

5. Secret Sisters: Every girl draws another girl's name out of a bag at the beginning of the season and gets her a small gift (like a candy bar or some nail polish) before each game. Sisters are revealed at the end of the season.

Face Painting

One sure way to show your spirit is to paint your face with your team or school colors. Face paint is easy and fun to make.

What you need:

- ★ Small bowls
- ★ Solid shortening
- ★ Cornstarch
- ★ Spoons
- ★ Baby powder
- ★ Cotton swabs or balls
- ★ Food coloring in school colors
- ★ New paintbrush
- ★ Small jars with lids
- ★ water

What you do:

1. In a small bowl, mix 1 1/2 tablespoons solid shortening and 3 tablespoons cornstarch. Stir. If mixture is too thick, add water one drop at a time.

2. Add food coloring and mix well.

3. Store in small, sealed jars.

4. Apply to the face using fingertips, cotton balls, swabs, or an unused paintbrush.

5. To prevent smudging, dab baby powder on top of the design.

CheerLEADERS

Can fans fire up a crowd the way cheerleaders can? Nope! All cheerleaders are great fans, but not all fans are cheerleaders. Why? It comes down to showmanship and sportsmanship 24/7! Most fans get frustrated when the team is losing. They give up and stop cheering. Some leave the game early. Not cheerleaders! Cheerleaders set good examples for

Face painting is a fun way to show your spirit.

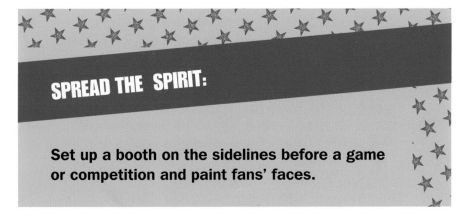

SPREAD THE SPIRIT:

Set up a booth on the sidelines before a game or competition and paint fans' faces.

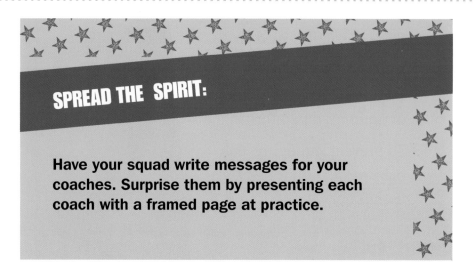

SPREAD THE SPIRIT:

Have your squad write messages for your coaches. Surprise them by presenting each coach with a framed page at practice.

fans. They keep fans cheering with their high energy and "never give up" attitude.

TIP: Sometimes a fan will start a chant or cheer. Join in!

Showmanship: Cheerleaders must let their spirit shine through their performance. It is your job to make the routines look sharp and polished. Good showmanship gets the crowd on their feet. It pumps up an audience. Be loud and act proud even when your team loses. Here are some ways to get the crowd to notice you. Once they do, your energy and enthusiasm will spread throughout the stands. In no time, you will have the crowds cheering with you!

- ★ Smile, smile, smile!

- ★ Keep your energy up. No one wants to watch a routine that fizzles halfway through the performance.

- ★ Look at the crowd or the judge. Cheer for them.

- ★ Project your voice. If the last row cannot hear you, you are not doing your job.

Fans at Baylor University show their enthusiasm.

★ Vary your chants and make them short and snappy. Include some that encourage fan participation.

Sportsmanship: It is easy to smile when your team is winning. It is easy to cheer when your dance routine gets high marks. But what happens when your team loses? What happens if you land on your backside? No one likes a sore loser. If you are a cheerleader, you smile and stay positive even when you have a tough day. You are a good sport. Sportsmanship is the way you act. It means you respect yourself, the other team, your teammates, and your

This cheerleader's sign leaves no doubt as to what spectators need to do.

coach. It means that you maintain a positive attitude even when you are disappointed.

Just ask Tracy Holzer:

SIMPLY BECAUSE WE DO NOT RUN ACROSS GOAL LINES, SLAM DUNK BASKETBALLS, OR HIT HOME RUNS DOESN'T MEAN WE CAN'T CHANGE THE SCORE.

> *After cheering in high school and college, I had my heart set on being a professional cheerleader. I tried out for the Sacramento Kings Cheerleaders. I danced and cheered my heart out and made it to the finals! Then, when it came time to perform the final choreography for the judges, I pulled a hamstring and couldn't finish. After all that hard work, I did not make the squad. Although disappointed, I congratulated all the other girls who made the squad. My true spirit carried me through with a winning attitude. I realized I was still a cheerleader whether I had the skirt or not.*

TIP: Cheer *for* your team, not *against* the other team.

TIP: Whether you win or lose, find something nice to say to your opponent.

SPREAD THE SPIRIT

If you host a game or a competition, make the other cheerleaders feel welcome. Wish them luck. Give them a basket filled with items they might need. Put hair gel, bobby pins, hairspray, powder, mints, hand lotion, ponytail holders, and a sewing kit inside.

Megaphones help cheerleaders project their voices.

2
SCORE WITH SPIRIT

In 1954, Lawrence "Herkie" Herkimer, founder of the National Cheerleaders Association, held a cheerleading camp. He gave out awards to teams who had the best jumps, stunts, and tumbling. But the team that impressed him the most that year was not as talented as the other squads. Their skills were weak. But they had something that no other team had: a spirit that could not be broken. They had a "can-do" attitude. Herkie felt they deserved an award for their spirit. He snapped a twig off of a tree and told them that they had won the first ever *spirit stick*.

Today, many coaches award the spirit stick after a practice or game to the cheerleader who had a winning attitude. Before it is returned at the next practice, she writes her name on it and adds a small trinket, such as a sticker or charm.

Make a Spirit Stick

Find an empty potato chip can or a paper towel roll. Cover it by rolling felt around it. Use your team colors. Add beans inside to make noise. Cover the ends with pom-poms. Your spirit stick is ready!

If you cannot make one, look for a twig on the ground. The girls can write their names on ribbons and tie them around the twig.

Congratulations!

Usually, the squad has a celebration at the end of the year. Help your coaches come up with awards. Everyone can win something. Here is a list to get you started:

★ Pom-pom Award (Most Spirited)

★ Banana Split Award (Best Split)

★ Superman Award (Fearless Flyer)

★ Nerves of Steel Award (Super Stunter)

★ Dance Diva (Best Dance Moves)

★ Can You Hear Me Now Award (Best Voice Projection)

Brainstorm more ideas with your teammates.

COMING TOGETHER IS A BEGINNING. KEEPING TOGETHER IS PROGRESS. WORKING TOGETHER IS SUCCESS.

HENRY FORD

Lollipop Cheerleaders

Awards can be certificates or trophies—or they can be things you make yourself, like this simple craft.

What you need: small lollipops, two pipe cleaners, small pom-pom craft balls, glue, paper, and marker

What you do: Wrap the pipe cleaners around the lollipop stick. Make arms and legs with the pipe cleaners. Glue or twist pom-poms onto the arms. Write an award on a piece of paper and glue it to the pom-pom.

SPREAD THE SPIRIT

Glue pins to the back of the lollipop cheerleader, attach a sign reading "#1 Fan," and pass out to people in the stands.

"You're a Gem" Locker Mirror

Is your coach looking for a way to recognize the entire squad for their achievements? Share this idea with her: Each girl gets a magnetic mirror. When the coach notices a cheerleader working extra hard, displaying good sportsmanship, or helping a teammate, she gives that person a gem (the plastic kind sold in packages in craft stores). The cheerleader glues the gem on her mirror. How many gems can each cheerleader earn throughout the year?

After lots of hard work, these cheerleaders have received trophies recognizing their achievements.

Get Involved!

Cheerleaders often perform at community events. Sometimes they march in parades and cheer on special holidays like July 4th and Veterans Day. Many squads volunteer to help out local charities or do community service activities. It helps the members bond as a team. It strengthens their friendships. But the best thing about it is that it lets teammates give back to the community that has supported them.

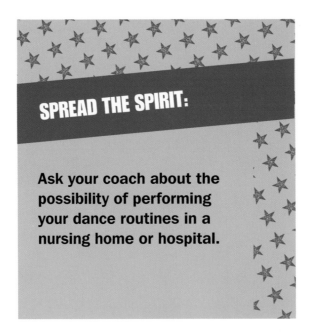

SPREAD THE SPIRIT:

Ask your coach about the possibility of performing your dance routines in a nursing home or hospital.

3
PUMP IT UP!

Some cheerleaders are on all-star squads. They compete against other squads, but they do not cheer for a team. If you are an all-star cheerleader, you may want to start a pep/spirit club in your school. You will get to spread your spirit all year long!

The pep club works closely with the school's cheerleaders. By working together, you can double the spirit and activities! Some schools require students to join the pep/spirit club before they can try out for cheerleading.

To start a club, you will need an advisor. An advisor is a teacher who will help you run the club. Next, make and hang posters describing the club. Once members sign up, have a meeting. All members and advisors should come. At this meeting, the group should brainstorm ways to increase school spirit.

Cheerleaders at practice. You can spread your spirit at school through a pep or spirit club.

Here are some ideas to get you started:

★ Have a door-decorating contest before a big game.

★ Make posters and hang them in the hallways.

★ Decorate a twenty-foot roll of paper for the team to run through at the game.

★ Pass out bubble gum with an attached card that says "Let's blow past the competition."

★ Make spirit bracelets in school colors.

★ Place index cards that read "Time to Beat the (team name)!" on every school clock.

★ Decorate T-shirts or tank tops with markers and puffy paint for game day.

★ Plan a "Stuff the Seats" night where you work extra hard to fill the stands with fans for a certain event.

Cheerleaders on the field at a football game. A pep club also encourages the school's teams.

Mascots fire up the crowd with their antics. This is the mascot of the UCLA Bruins.

Once your club is established, it is time to consider a mascot if your school does not have one. Mascots are people who wear costumes, act silly, dance, and rev up the crowd. They entertain the crowd. They help get the fans to chant and cheer for the team. The mascot must be a hard worker and have lots of energy. It has to be someone who likes to be in the spotlight and is not shy. The only thing a mascot cannot do is talk! Instead, mascots communicate through dancing and gestures. Sometimes they will join the cheerleaders in easy stunts.

The Ohio State mascot, Brutus the Buckeye, signs autographs. Mascots have to communicate without speech or facial expressions.

Mascots try out for the position. To be fair, each person who auditions wears a costume so no one knows who it is. Sometimes a cheerleader wants to try something new. She might want a change and decide that she would rather be the school mascot. If you are thinking about trying out, here are some tips:

★ Videotape yourself acting silly and having fun with friends. How did you do?

★ Have friends call out different emotions and act them out. Can you act surprised? Sad? Happy? Embarrassed? All while wearing a costume?

★ Go to a sporting event and watch how a mascot interacts with the crowd.

★ Practice your best dance moves.

★ Create a short skit to perform during your tryout.

★ Create a funny entrance and a signature move.

TIP: What if your school does not have a costume for the mascot? Ask around and find someone who sews to make one. Be sure to thank them!

SPREAD THE SPIRIT:

Your club will need money to buy craft materials and giveaways. Talk to your advisor about raising money for the club. Fundraising activities are a great way to boost school spirit because everyone works together. Can you think up some creative ways to raise money?

4 PEP RALLIES

Pep clubs and cheerleaders often work together to boost the morale and spirit of the school. Pep rallies are a fun way to spread the spirit. Cheerleaders are always involved in pep rallies. They help plan them. A pep rally helps to get the school fired up about a big game or an upcoming season.

Why have pep rallies? Besides boosting morale, rallies teach the crowds chants and cheers, and they reinforce what sportsmanship is. Pep rallies are usually held in school, and there are several throughout the year. Some schools have one for each season. This way, no sport teams or clubs are left out.

To have a successful pep rally, it must be organized. All students should be invited to participate. Music sets the tone. If you have a marching band, it is the perfect chance for the

Cheerleaders know how to spread the spirit! Here, a squad performs in a South Carolina school.

members to show off! Here are some tips to think about as you plan your first rally:

★ It should not be longer than 25–30 minutes.

★ High energy is a must. You want to feel the excitement.

★ Crowd involvement through games and skits is key.

★ Involve the whole student body.

★ Find an emcee who is funny and can keep it moving along.

A pep rally is a good place to show off the marching band.

A pep rally at Iowa State. Introducing the team and coaches is an important part of the program.

★ Pick simple themes like Beach Day or Hat Day to unite the student body.

★ Run through the pep rally routine a few times to work out kinks.

★ Create a checklist of items needed: chairs, microphones, prizes, props, contest/game materials, etc.

TIP: Once you have a schedule, save it and use it for future rallies. Vary the cheers and games to keep it fresh.

SPREAD THE SPIRIT

A pep rally is the perfect time to hand out extra megaphones, pom-poms, and signs to fans.

A sample schedule:

1. The Marching Band: Plays school song and at least one other song that is easy identifiable, such as *We Will Rock You* by Queen.

2. Cheerleaders: Come out tumbling and introduce a few chants that the crowd recognizes.

3. Emcee: Welcomes everyone and fires up the crowd with a short speech. Should mention a game or upcoming event.

4. Pep Club: Announces winners of schoolwide contest.

5. Emcee: Introduces coaches.

6. Contest/game (see below).

7. Band: Plays fight song or school song.

8. Cheerleaders: Teach new chant.

9. Emcee: Reviews good sportsmanship. If possible, gives examples.

10. Skit (should involve pep club members, teachers, athletes).

11. Contest/game.

12. Emcee: Closing remarks.

13. Cheerleaders: Wow the crowd with final dance routine.

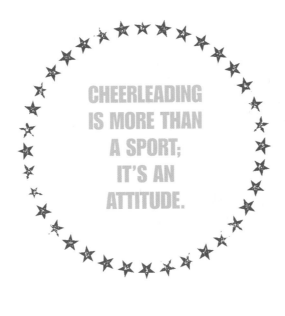

CHEERLEADING IS MORE THAN A SPORT; IT'S AN ATTITUDE.

Contests/Games for Pep Rally

★ *Audience Art:* Select random students from the stands. Give them a box of materials to create a spirit poster/display. After five minutes, have the crowd vote for their favorite. (Pep rally schedule continues while students make posters.)

★ *Head to Toe:* Select ten kids out of the crowd. Pair them up. One person in each pair wraps streamers around the other person. The team to wrap

These high school cheerleaders in Connecticut use a peppy chant to inspire fans.

WITHOUT
A CONDUCTOR
THERE IS NO
ORCHESTRA. WITHOUT
CHEERLEADERS
IT'S ONLY A GAME.

the person from head to toe first—with no skin or clothes showing—wins a prize.

TIP: If you are in high school, pick two kids from each grade and face off: freshmen, sophomores, juniors, and seniors. Pick two teachers as well.

★ *Nosedive:* Pick a grade level per rally. Hand out paper to the kids. They must make a paper airplane and write their name on it. When a whistle blows, they try to hit the target in the middle of the gym. The one who is closest wins a prize.

★ *Balloon Buster:* Grab twenty kids from the crowd. Tie a balloon to each person's ankle. All players stand in a marked area. Each person tries to pop other people's balloons. The last person with an unpopped balloon wins a prize.

Ohio State University cheerleaders keep the crowd's spirits high.

Chants for Pep Rally

A chant is a short, peppy cheer. It is repeated several times.
Arm and leg motions emphasize the beat of the words.
Chants are easy to remember so the fans will chant with you.
Add motions and try these at your next pep rally:

1. *Yell for the [team name].*
    We can't be beat.
    If you want to win,
    Stomp your feet!

A good chant will inspire the crowd to join in.

2. *It's spirit time.*
   It's all the time.
   We've come to cheer.
   We're glad you're here.

3. *Let's hear it for spirit!*
   Stand tall and proud.
   Let's hear it for spirit!
   Shout extra loud! SPIRIT!

4. *Let's go [team name], Let's go! (clap clap)*

5. *Let's get fired up! (clap, clap, clap, clap, clap)*
   We are fired up! (clap, clap, clap, clap, clap)

TIP: Pom-poms or foam fingers are fun, inexpensive prizes.

Now that you've got spirit, spread it. As they say in cheerleading, bring it on! May the spirit be with you!

EAT.
SLEEP.
CHEER.
REPEAT.

WORDS TO KNOW

all-star team—Squads of cheerleaders who compete with other squads instead of cheering for a sports team.

chant—A short, peppy cheer, repeated several times.

mascot—A costumed character or animal that represents a sports team. Mascots appear at games to encourage team spirit.

morale—The level of enthusiasm, confidence, and positive attitude in a person or group.

pep club or spirit club—A school club whose goal is to increase school spirit.

pep rally—An event held for the whole student body to build school spirit. It can include games, skits, cheers, contests, and songs.

pom-poms—Fluffy, colored balls made out of plastic or paper.

stunt—An activity that involves lifting or throwing a cheerleader.

LEARN MORE

BOOKS

Carrier, Justin, and Donna McKay. *Complete Cheerleading.* Champaign, Ill.: Human Kinetics, 2006.

Jones, Jen. *Cheer Spirit: Revving Up the Crowd.* Mankato, Minn.: Capstone Press, 2006.

Jones, Jen. *Cheer Squad: Building Spirit and Getting Along.* Mankato, Minn.: Capstone Press, 2006.

Singer, Lynn. *Cheerleading.* New York: Rosen, 2007.

WEB SITES

Activity TV: Cheerleading
<http://www.activitytv.com/cheerleading-for-kids>

American Youth Football and Cheer
<http://www.americanyouthfootball.com/
cheerleading.asp>

Varsity Official Site
<http://www.varsity.com >

INDEX